A CONVERSATION WITH CRYSTALS: UNDERSTANDING CRYSTAL THERAPY

Energetic Interactions for Balance and Harmony

D.R. T Stephens

S.D.N Publishing

ISBN: 9798857210369

Cover design by: Art Painter
Library of Congress Control Number: 2018675309
Printed in the United States of America

CONTENTS

GENERAL DISCLAIMER

This book is intended to provide general information to the reader on the topics covered. The author and publisher have made every effort to ensure that the information herein is accurate and up-to-date at the time of publication. However, they do not warrant or guarantee the accuracy, completeness, adequacy, or currency of the information contained in this book. The author and publisher expressly disclaim any liability or responsibility for any errors or omissions in the content herein.

The information, guidance, advice, tips, and suggestions provided in this book are not intended to replace professional advice or consultation. Readers are strongly encouraged to consult with an appropriate professional for specific advice tailored to their situation before making any decisions or taking any actions based on the content of this book.

The views and opinions expressed in this book are those of the author and do not necessarily reflect the official policy or position of any other agency, organization, employer or company.

The author and publisher are not responsible for any actions taken or not taken by the reader based on the information, advice, or suggestions provided in this book. The reader is solely responsible for their actions and the consequences thereof.

This book is not intended to be a source of legal, business, medical or psychological advice, and readers are cautioned to seek the services of a competent professional in these or other areas of expertise.

All product names, logos, and brands are property of their respective owners. All company, product and service names used in this book are for identification purposes only. Use of these names, logos, and brands does not imply endorsement.

Readers of this book are advised to do their own due diligence when it comes to making decisions and all information, products, services and advice that have been provided should be independently verified by your own qualified professionals.

By reading this book, you agree that the author and publisher are not responsible for your success or failure resulting from any information presented in this book.

CHAPTER 1: INTRODUCTION TO CRYSTAL THERAPY: A TIMELESS CONNECTION

From the vibrant streets of Manhattan to the serene valleys of the Himalayas, crystals have found a cherished place in the hearts of millions. Their shimmering hues and alluring structures have fascinated us for generations, yet it's their intangible energy that forms an invisible bond between humans and the Earth's treasures. Welcome to the world of crystal therapy—a realm where stones communicate without words and healing happens through vibrations.

Have you ever picked up a smooth, cool stone and felt an immediate sense of peace? Or perhaps you've been drawn to the vibrant colors of a crystal in a jewelry store, feeling an inexplicable connection? This isn't mere coincidence; it's the beginning of a dialogue, a conversation with crystals.

The Earth, in its boundless generosity, has bestowed upon us a plethora of these gems, each with its unique energetic fingerprint.

From the deep purples of amethysts that resonate with our intuition, to the clear, prismatic beams of quartz that amplify our thoughts, crystals serve as tangible reminders of the Earth's long, intricate history and the cosmic dance of molecules.

But what exactly is crystal therapy? In its simplest form, it's the art and science of employing these crystalline structures to promote physical, emotional, and spiritual well-being. Think of them as conduits—channels that bridge the gap between the Earth's grounding energies and our bustling human experiences.

Historically, many ancient civilizations, from the wise Egyptians to the intuitive Mayans, recognized the power of these stones. They didn't have electron microscopes or advanced spectral analysis tools, but they had an innate understanding—an intuitive grasp of the healing potential of crystals. In tombs, in ceremonies, and in daily life, crystals were revered not just as ornamental pieces but as integral tools for balance and harmony.

Modern science might be catching up, with studies delving into the piezoelectric properties of some crystals or their ability to store information, but for many, their appeal remains mystical, deeply personal, and profoundly healing.

You see, every crystal has its story—a journey from the depths of the Earth, undergoing intense pressure, heat, and transformation to emerge as the gleaming gem it becomes. Much like us, they bear the scars and beauty of their histories. And much like us, they seek connection, resonance, and purpose.

As we embark on this enlightening journey together, you'll be introduced to the silent language of crystals. A language that doesn't rely on words but thrives on energies and frequencies.

Together, we'll demystify the age-old practices, equip you with knowledge, and perhaps most importantly, encourage you to listen—to hold a crystal close and hear the whispers of the Earth and the echoes of the cosmos.

So, whether you're a seasoned gemologist, a curious skeptic, or someone seeking alternative paths to well-being, there's a place for you in this conversation. After all, at the heart of crystal therapy lies a universal truth—that we are all interconnected, a symphony of energies seeking harmony. And as you'll soon discover, with crystals by our side, we're never truly alone on this quest.

CHAPTER 2: THE SCIENCE BEHIND THE STONES: ENERGETIC FOUNDATIONS

There's an irresistible allure to the shimmering beauty of crystals. Their facets catch the light, scattering rainbows, drawing many to marvel at their external elegance. But the true magic of these natural wonders lies beneath the surface, in their very molecular makeup and the invisible dance of energy they conduct. This chapter peels back the glossy veneer and delves deep into the fascinating science behind the stones. Let's embark on a journey into the core of crystals!

Atoms, Molecules, and More!

Atoms are the essential constituents of matter, and they can be found in every crystal, whether it be a dazzling diamond or a simple quartz. Atoms are incredibly small particles. These atoms bind together to form molecules, and it's the specific arrangement of these molecules that gives each crystal its unique structure and properties.

Picture a bustling dance floor with dancers (atoms) moving in synchronized patterns (molecular arrangements). In the world of crystals, this dance is not just metaphorical but quite literal. At the atomic level, particles vibrate, creating a frequency. This frequency, or vibration, is a significant aspect of the crystal's energetic profile.

Piezoelectricity: The Power of Pressure

A fascinating property of some crystals, like quartz, is piezoelectricity. This term might sound complex, but it's a concept that's beautifully simple. When mechanical pressure is applied to these crystals, they generate an electrical charge. This discovery has revolutionized industries, leading to the creation of items like quartz wristwatches. But in the realm of healing and energy work, it highlights the responsiveness of crystals to external stimuli, suggesting that our interactions with them can indeed create energetic shifts.

Vibrational Frequencies: The Song of the Stones

Everything in the universe vibrates—trees, animals, humans, and of course, crystals. These vibrations, or frequencies, form the basis of the energetic exchanges we experience with the world around us. While we might not hear it with our ears, each crystal sings its unique song, a vibrational tune that can align, enhance, or even shift our own energetic frequencies.

Crystals and Energy Fields

Research has suggested that our bodies have electromagnetic fields, often referred to as auras. Crystals, with their unique vibrational frequencies, can interact with these fields. Have you ever walked into a room and felt an inexplicable energy, be it positive or heavy? Crystals act as modulators, helping cleanse, amplify, or stabilize these energies.

Harnessing the Healing

Modern medicine increasingly recognizes the role of vibrational therapies, from ultrasound to laser treatments. Crystals, in their natural form, can be viewed as tools for vibrational healing. By resonating with our body's energy centers (which we'll explore in depth later), they can help restore balance where there's discord and amplify harmony where it exists.

It's crucial, however, to approach the topic with an open heart and a discerning mind. The science of crystals is still a field of ongoing research and discovery. While many anecdotes and traditions vouch for their healing prowess, it's essential to understand and respect the balance between empirical science and experiential wisdom.

In conclusion, while the radiant beauty of crystals can be captivating, their true marvel lies deep within, in the dance of atoms, the song of frequencies, and the silent conversations they have with our energies. They are not just inert rocks but dynamic entities, pulsating with life and energy. And as we delve deeper into this book, we'll learn to harness this energy, transforming our lives and spaces with the harmonious embrace of Earth's treasures.

CHAPTER 3: HISTORICAL PERSPECTIVES: CRYSTAL HEALING ACROSS CULTURES AND AGES

Crystals have been enchanting humans for millennia. Their glittering appearance and unique properties have ensured that they've remained objects of intrigue and admiration, with civilizations across the globe using them for various purposes. In this chapter, we journey back in time, tracing the footsteps of our ancestors to unearth the rich tapestry of crystal lore that has shaped human history.

The Ancients and Their Treasures

1. Egypt: The land of pyramids and pharaohs, ancient Egypt held crystals in high regard. Lapis lazuli, with its deep celestial blue, adorned the jewelry of royalty, believed to provide protection and guidance in the afterlife. Turquoise and carnelian, other beloved gems, were worn as amulets to ward off evil and attract prosperity.

2. India: Historical texts such as the Vedas, dating back over 5,000 years, mention the use of crystals in rituals and ceremonies. The revered ruby, symbolizing the sun, was believed to protect its wearer from enemies.

3. China: For the Chinese, jade held a special place. In addition to being a symbol of social prestige, it was also considered to represent a connection between the physical world and the spiritual realms. Because of this, it was incorporated into the burial garb of royalty to ensure their safe passage and protection in the hereafter.

4. Ancient Greece: They believed that clear quartz was actually water that had frozen so deeply that it would always remain solid, which is where the word "crystal" comes from; the Greek word "krustallos," which means "ice," is where the word "crystal" originates. Amethyst, on the other hand, was worn to prevent intoxication—its name translates to 'not intoxicated'.

Medieval Times and the Magic of Minerals

In medieval Europe, crystals were often associated with healing. Hildegard of Bingen, a renowned Benedictine abbess, wrote extensively on the medicinal properties of gems. She believed, for instance, that sapphire could help treat leprosy, while amethyst could calm the mind.

The New World and Crystal Curiosities

Native American tribes, like the Hopi and the Zuni, had their own crystal stories. They carved animal fetishes from different stones, each representing specific attributes and powers. Clear quartz, for instance, was deemed a gift from the Earth Mother, a tool to communicate with the spiritual realm.

Modern Resurgence

Though the allure of crystals never truly faded, the 20th century saw a global resurgence in their popularity, particularly within the New Age movement. Their potential as tools for meditation, healing, and spiritual growth was revisited and embraced anew.

Across Borders and Beyond Time

While each culture had its own unique relationship and understanding of crystals, some universal themes resonate. Protection, healing, spiritual guidance—no matter where or when, these are human desires that have consistently found an ally in crystals. They are testament to an intuitive understanding, an ancient knowing, that there's more to these beautiful stones than meets the eye.

Today, in our tech-driven era, one might wonder if these age-old beliefs hold water. But remember, just as our ancestors looked to the stars for answers, they also looked to the earth, finding solace in its treasures. As science advances, it often merges with, rather than diverges from, ancient wisdom. The electromagnetic properties of crystals, for instance, are being researched for various technological applications.

In the embrace of a crystal, we are not just holding a piece of the earth; we are holding a piece of history, an ancient memory, a testament to the timeless dance between mankind and nature. So, the next time you find yourself marveling at the sparkle of a gem, remember the countless hands it has passed through, the myriad tales it could tell, and the universal energies it channels.

CHAPTER 4: UNDERSTANDING CRYSTAL VIBRATIONS: HOW THEY RESONATE WITH US

Have you ever pondered the concept of resonance? Imagine striking a tuning fork and holding it next to another. The second fork, untouched by you, begins to hum in harmony with the first. This is resonance – the response of one object to the vibrations of another. Crystals, with their unique structures and compositions, resonate in their own characteristic ways. And fascinatingly enough, these vibrations can harmonize beautifully with our own energetic frequencies.

Nature's Song: The Vibrations of Crystals

Each crystal, depending on its composition, structure, and color, vibrates at a specific frequency. These vibrations arise due to the regular and repeating arrangement of atoms and molecules within the crystal. It's like nature's own symphony, with each crystal contributing its distinctive note.

Our Personal Frequencies: How We Vibrate

Humans, too, are vibratory beings. Each of our cells, tissues, and organs, and more abstractly, our thoughts, emotions, and intentions, generate their own vibrational frequencies. Together, they form a complex harmonic that is as unique as a fingerprint.

When we are in a state of health and well-being, our personal symphony plays harmoniously. However, life's challenges can throw our frequencies into discord. Stress, trauma, and negative thought patterns can alter our inner music, leading to energetic imbalances and, eventually, physical and emotional ailments.

The Dance of Resonance

When we introduce a crystal into our personal space, be it through wearing, holding, or meditating with it, its vibrations can interact with ours. If the crystal's frequency aligns well with a frequency that our body, mind, or spirit needs, resonance occurs.

In the presence of this resonant frequency, our own imbalanced or disharmonious vibrations can begin to shift, moving towards balance and harmony. This is the foundation of crystal healing: using the stable and consistent vibrations of crystals to inspire our own energies to realign and heal.

Fine-tuning with Intention

Our thoughts and intentions carry their own powerful vibrations. When combined with the consistent frequencies of crystals, we can amplify our intentions, directing our energies more purposefully. By selecting a crystal whose vibrations align with our intentions, we create a powerful energetic partnership, enabling profound shifts within ourselves.

An Empirical Perspective

While the energetic interactions between humans and crystals have long been recognized in various traditions, modern science is also beginning to acknowledge the vibrational properties of crystals. One visible illustration of the vibrational features of crystals is the phenomenon known as piezoelectricity, which occurs when some crystals create voltage in response to the application of mechanical stress. Devices like quartz watches, which utilize the consistent vibration of quartz crystals, are everyday testaments to the measurable frequencies of these stones.

In Closing

The magical world of crystals offers us a chance to harmonize with the Earth's energies, to find balance and resonance in our lives. While the idea of vibrating energies might seem esoteric to some, it's truly a fundamental aspect of both our nature and the universe at large. As we venture deeper into the world of crystal therapy, understanding this resonance is key. By appreciating the dance of frequencies between ourselves and our crystal allies, we unlock a world of healing, transformation, and profound connection. So, next time you hold a crystal, close your eyes, and feel – truly feel – the gentle hum of the universe, and the loving song it sings just for you.

CHAPTER 5: CHOOSING YOUR CRYSTAL ALLIES: SELECTING THE RIGHT STONES FOR YOUR NEEDS

In the vast world of gemstones and minerals, the kaleidoscope of colors, shapes, and energies can be both wondrous and overwhelming. Just as we find ourselves drawn to specific colors, scents, or places, our intuition often nudges us toward certain crystals. But how do we navigate this vibrant world and choose the right crystal allies for our unique journeys?

Tuning into Your Needs

Before diving into the myriad of available crystals, take a moment to reflect on your current state of being. Are you seeking solace, healing, invigoration, or clarity? Recognizing and acknowledging your needs is the first step in choosing the perfect crystal ally.

Crystal Color and Its Influence

Colors aren't just a visual delight. They vibrate at specific frequencies and influence our emotions and psyche. Here's a simple guide to understanding the essence of colors:

Reds (e.g., Garnet, Ruby): Represent passion, vitality, and grounding.

Oranges (e.g., Carnelian, Sunstone): Invoke creativity, confidence, and emotional balance.

Yellows (e.g., Citrine, Yellow Calcite): Enhance personal power, joy, and optimism.

Greens (e.g., Aventurine, Malachite): Promote healing, abundance, and love.

Blues (e.g., Aquamarine, Lapis Lazuli): Bring calm, communication, and introspection.

Violets & Purples (e.g., Amethyst, Charoite): Foster spiritual growth, intuition, and tranquility.

Clear (e.g., Clear Quartz, Selenite): Amplify energy, clarity, and consciousness.

Blacks (e.g., Obsidian, Black Tourmaline): Offer protection, grounding, and absorption of negativity.

Connecting with the Crystal

Once you have an idea of what you're seeking, visit a local crystal shop. Allow yourself to explore freely. Notice if any stones call out to you. When you're drawn to a crystal, hold it in your hand. Close your eyes and feel its energy. Does it soothe, excite, ground, or elevate you? Trust your intuition.

Research and Resonance

While intuition is a powerful guide, complementing it with knowledge is essential. Upon selecting a potential crystal ally, delve into its historical and metaphysical properties. Many cultures have held beliefs and traditions regarding specific stones. Cross-referencing your personal feelings with established information can be incredibly affirming.

Consider Your Application

How you intend to use the crystal can also guide your choice. For example, if you're looking to enhance meditation, a calming stone like Amethyst might be ideal. If you're embarking on a new venture and need motivation, the fiery energy of Citrine could be your ally.

Personalizing Your Crystal Collection

Over time, you'll find that your collection grows. Each stone, with its unique energy and story, can cater to various aspects of your life journey. Remember that as you evolve, so too might your affinity with different crystals. Periodically reassessing your collection and attuning to new stones keeps your energetic interactions fresh and relevant.

A Gentle Reminder

Crystals can be an incredible source of support; nevertheless, they are not a substitute for the advice or treatment offered by a qualified medical practitioner. They serve as harmonious tools, accompanying our journey towards balance and well-being.

Embarking on the Journey

As you begin, or continue, your exploration of crystals, cherish each discovery. In this wondrous realm, every stone holds a universe of energy, waiting to resonate with yours. By tuning in, researching, and trusting both your intuition and the wisdom of the ages, you'll find the perfect crystal allies to accompany you on your life's journey. Remember, in the world of crystals, the journey itself is as enriching as the destination. Embrace it with an open heart and an eager spirit.

CHAPTER 6: THE CHAKRA SYSTEM: CRYSTALS FOR BALANCING ENERGY CENTERS

The human body is a masterpiece, not just of anatomy but also of energy. These energy centers, often referred to as 'chakras', have been recognized by various ancient cultures and modern holistic practices alike. These vibrant vortexes interact with our physical, emotional, and spiritual selves, and guess what? Crystals, with their distinct vibrational frequencies, can assist in harmonizing and balancing these chakras!

Understanding the Chakra System

"Chakra" is a Sanskrit term that translates to "wheel" or "disk." Imagine that your body is filled with energy wheels that spin from the bottom of your spine all the way up to the top of your head. There are seven basic chakras, and each one is associated with a different set of organs, feelings, and aspects of one's spiritual being.

Root Chakra (Muladhara): Positioned at the very bottom of the backbone. It is connected to experiences of safety and grounding, as well as our fundamental requirements.

Sacral Chakra (Svadhishthana): Situated below the navel. It connects with our emotions, desires, and creativity.

Solar Plexus Chakra (Manipura): Positioned above the navel. It relates to our self-worth, confidence, and power.

Heart Chakra (Anahata): Centered in the chest. It symbolizes love, joy, and inner peace.

Throat Chakra (Vishuddha): Found in the throat. It stands for communication, expression, and truth.

Third Eye Chakra (Ajna): Located between the eyebrows. It pertains to intuition, imagination, and wisdom.

Crown Chakra (Sahasrara): Positioned on the top of the head. It connects with our spiritual connection and universal consciousness.

Crystals for Each Chakra

The vibrational frequencies of crystals can resonate with specific chakras, helping to restore balance and unblock energy flows.

Root Chakra: Red Jasper and Hematite can offer grounding energies.

Sacral Chakra: Carnelian and Orange Calcite promote emotional balance and creativity.

Solar Plexus Chakra: Citrine and Yellow Jasper boost self-confidence and personal power.

Heart Chakra: Rose Quartz and Green Aventurine encourage love, compassion, and healing.

Throat Chakra: Blue Lace Agate and Sodalite enhance communication and self-expression.

Third Eye Chakra: Amethyst and Lapis Lazuli can aid intuition and clarity.

Crown Chakra: Clear Quartz and Selenite foster spiritual growth and divine connection.

Balancing Your Chakras with Crystals

Crystal Meditation: Place the chosen crystal on its corresponding chakra while meditating. Visualize its energy interacting with the chakra, restoring balance and harmony.

Wearing Chakra Jewelry: Adorning yourself with chakra jewelry allows the crystal's energy to continuously resonate with your energy centers.

Crystal Beds: Lying on a bed or mat infused with chakra crystals can provide an immersive healing experience.

Elixirs: Some (but not all!) crystals can be safely used to make elixirs, infusing water with their essence.

Remember: Safety First

While crystal therapy can be a wonderful tool for chakra balancing, always ensure you're using stones safely. Not all crystals should be ingested or come into direct prolonged contact with the skin. Also, while crystals offer beautiful supportive energy, they're complementary to traditional healthcare and should not replace medical treatments or therapies.

Your Unique Energetic Blueprint

Everyone's energy system is unique. Some might have overactive chakras, while others could have underactive ones. Using crystals, you can gently and lovingly nurture these energy centers back into harmony. By understanding your own needs and applying the supportive energies of the right crystals, you can pave the way for a balanced, vibrant, and harmonious existence.

CHAPTER 7: CLEANSING AND CHARGING: PREPARING YOUR CRYSTALS FOR USE

Ah, the feeling of holding a freshly acquired crystal—its raw energy, its pristine beauty, and the sensation of Earth's vibration in your palm. But, just like a new dress needs a wash before wearing or a musical instrument requires tuning before playing, your crystal also needs some prepping. Let's delve into the vital steps of cleansing and charging your crystalline companions, ensuring they're primed to assist you on your healing journey.

Why Cleanse Your Crystals?

Imagine this: crystals, much like sponges, absorb energies from their environment. Whether it's from the Earth, the hands that have handled them, or even the energies from places they've been stored, crystals can gather a medley of vibrations. By cleansing them, we ensure they're free from any unwanted energies and are reset to their natural state.

Methods for Cleansing Crystals:

Water: Holding your crystals under running water (preferably natural sources like a stream or river) can wash away negativity. However, do note, not all crystals like water—some can dissolve or get damaged. Stones like selenite and malachite are best kept dry.

Moonlight: Bathing your crystals under the gentle glow of moonlight, especially during a full moon, can purify and re-energize them.

Sunlight: Some crystals, like clear quartz or amethyst, can be revitalized with the sun's energy. However, prolonged exposure might fade their colors, so a brief sunbath is advisable.

Sound: Using sound frequencies from tuning forks, singing bowls, or even a resonating chant can clear unwanted energies.

Smoke: Sage, palo santo, or incense can be used to smudge your crystals, ensuring they're energetically cleansed.

Salt: Placing crystals on a bed of sea salt or Himalayan salt can purify them. Just remember, salt can be abrasive, so be gentle.

Other Crystals: Some crystals like selenite and clear quartz have the unique ability to cleanse other crystals. Simply placing your crystal beside or on them can do the trick.

Charging: Infusing Your Crystals with Intent

After cleansing, charging your crystals means setting an intention, thereby programming them to assist you in a specific manner.

Direct Energy: Holding your crystal close to your heart or third eye, visualize or speak your intention, allowing your energy to seep into the stone.

Earth: Burying your crystal in the soil lets it tap into the Earth's vibrational frequency, rejuvenating it.

Affirmations: Speaking positive affirmations or intentions over your crystals can program them with that specific energy.

Maintaining the Purity

Remember, frequent usage or a change in the crystal's texture, luminosity, or energy might indicate the need for another cleansing session. It's akin to taking a bath; just as our bodies need regular cleaning, so do our crystalline friends.

Trust Your Intuition

Throughout this process, your intuition is your guiding star. If a method feels right, it probably is. If a crystal seems like it needs cleansing or charging—even if you've just done it—listen to that inner nudge.

There's a beautiful relationship that unfolds when we care for our crystals. This mutual exchange of energy amplifies the bond, ensuring that every interaction resonates with love, respect, and purpose. As you invest time in preparing your crystals, you'll find that they, in turn, invest in your journey toward balance and harmony.

CHAPTER 8: CRYSTAL LAYOUTS: PATTERNS FOR HEALING AND MEDITATION

Crystals are more than just delightful treasures to look at; they are conduits for energetic transformation. When aligned in certain patterns or layouts, their power multiplies, creating a harmonious environment for healing and meditation. Let's embark on the journey of understanding how these layouts work and how to harness them in your quest for inner peace and wellness.

Why Use Crystal Layouts?

The arrangement of crystals in specific patterns allows for focused energy flow. Think of them like notes in a musical piece —each has its unique tone, but when combined, they produce a harmonious melody. Similarly, when crystals are thoughtfully positioned, their energies interact, producing an enhanced vibrational field.

Popular Crystal Layouts for Healing and Meditation:

The Crystal Grid: A geometric pattern of energetically aligned stones charged by intention. Popular shapes include the Seed of Life, Flower of Life, or the Sri Yantra. The center stone, often the largest, anchors the energy, while surrounding stones radiate it outwards.

Chakra Layout: Aligning crystals with the seven major chakras (energy centers) of the body. This layout aids in balancing and cleansing the chakras, promoting overall well-being. For instance, amethyst might be placed on the crown chakra, while rose quartz could rest on the heart.

Circular or Spiral Layout: Representing cycles and wholeness, this layout is beneficial for understanding life's patterns and drawing energies inward or radiating them outwards.

Linear Layout: Often used for directing energy flow in one direction. Useful for clearing blockages or channeling energy from the head to the feet or vice versa.

Creating Your Own Layouts:

As with everything in the realm of crystals, personal intuition is paramount. Here's a simple guide to creating a layout that resonates with you:

Purpose: Start by understanding the intention behind the layout. Is it for stress relief? Spiritual connection? Healing a specific ailment?

Choosing Crystals: Based on your purpose, select crystals that resonate with your goal. Reference earlier chapters for guidance on choosing the right stone allies.

Location: Decide where you'll be setting up your layout—on a table, on the floor, or even on your body during meditation.

Arrangement: Begin by placing the primary crystal (often the largest or most significant) and then arrange others around it. Trust your intuition—there's no wrong layout. Feel the energy and adjust as necessary.

Activation: Once satisfied, take a moment to activate the layout with your intention. This can be done by hovering your hand over the layout, envisioning a bright light connecting each stone, or even using a crystal wand to trace pathways between them.

After the Session:

Once your meditation or healing session concludes, it's essential to cleanse the crystals, as they've absorbed and transmuted energies. Refer to our earlier chapter on "Cleansing and Charging" for guidance.

In Conclusion:

Crystal layouts are a transformative tool in the realm of crystal therapy. They provide a structured, amplified energy field tailored to specific needs, magnifying the inherent power of each stone. While traditional layouts offer time-tested benefits, creating your personalized arrangement can be equally potent. Always remember: intention is key. With a clear purpose and an open heart, the crystals will effortlessly guide you on your path to healing and balance.

CHAPTER 9:
ELIXIRS AND GRIDS:
AMPLIFYING THE
POWER OF CRYSTALS

Imagine walking into a serene room where a mesmerizing grid of crystals lies shimmering on a table, their energies interweaving in harmony. Beside it, a sunlit jar holds water infused with the essence of a special crystal. This is the magical world of crystal elixirs and grids, pathways that amplify the power of our crystal friends.

Crystal Elixirs: Nature's Liquid Healing

A crystal elixir is essentially water that has imbibed the vibrational essence of a crystal. It's a way of internalizing the beneficial frequencies of the stones.

How to Make a Crystal Elixir:

Choosing Your Crystal: This step can't be overstated. Some crystals can be toxic when immersed in water, so always ensure your chosen stone is safe for consumption. Amethyst, rose quartz, and clear quartz are popular choices.

Cleansing the Crystal: Before it touches water, make sure your crystal is energetically and physically cleansed.

Preparing the Elixir: Place the cleansed crystal in a glass jar filled with pure water. Let it sit under sunlight for a few hours or under moonlight overnight. The sun or moon's rays will help transfer the crystal's energy to the water.

Strain and Store: Once energized, you can transfer the elixir to a drinking bottle. Keep it refrigerated to maintain its freshness.

Usage: Sip the elixir throughout the day. As you drink, take a moment to connect with your intention and the energy of the crystal.

Crystal Grids: Networks of Energetic Synergy

A crystal grid is an intentional arrangement of stones that work together to manifest a particular goal or intention. The combined energies of the crystals create a powerful vibratory field.

Steps to Create a Crystal Grid:

Intention Setting: Your grid's purpose can range from attracting abundance, enhancing intuition, or fostering love. Clarifying this intention is the foundational step.

Selecting Crystals: Depending on your goal, choose crystals that align with that energy. For instance, citrine can be great for abundance, while sodalite may enhance intuition.

Grid Foundation: This is typically a geometric pattern printed or drawn on a cloth or paper. Sacred geometry patterns, like the Flower of Life or Metatron's Cube, are favorites among crystal enthusiasts.

Placing the Stones: Start from the outside, working your way inward. The central stone, known as the "Master Crystal," serves as an anchor, collecting and unifying the energy of the surrounding crystals.

Activating the Grid: Using a clear quartz point or wand, connect the crystals by drawing invisible lines between them, envisioning them energetically linking up. As you do this, hold your intention firmly in mind.

The Synergy of Elixirs and Grids:

Both elixirs and grids tap into the collective energies of multiple crystals. While elixirs allow for a more personal, internal experience, grids radiate their powerful energies into spaces, benefiting everyone present. Combining the two — by using an elixir during a grid meditation session, for example — can create a beautifully heightened experience.

Embracing the Liquid and Lattice:

Crystal elixirs and grids are two incredible avenues to deepen our bond with the crystalline kingdom. Elixirs bring the vibrational essence of the stones into our very being, while grids envelop us in a comforting blanket of their combined energies. As with all crystal practices, the key lies in intention and reverence. Approach with an open heart, and these crystalline allies will surely guide you toward balance, harmony, and profound transformation.

CHAPTER 10: CRYSTALS FOR EMOTIONAL HEALING: FROM HEARTBREAK TO JOY

Ah, the kaleidoscope of human emotions! They paint our world with vibrant colors and shades. But at times, emotional pain can cloud our existence. Here's where our sparkling allies — crystals — play a transformative role, gently guiding us from emotional despair to vibrant joy.

Crystals: Nature's Emotional Balm

Crystals harbor energies that resonate with our emotional selves. They serve as mirrors reflecting our innermost feelings, helping us recognize, understand, and heal from emotional wounds.

The Connection of Crystals to Emotions:

The beauty of crystals goes beyond their physical allure. Their complex lattice structures absorb, amplify, and emit energy, interacting harmoniously with our emotional bodies. When matched with an appropriate emotion, they offer support, clarity, and healing.

Crystals for Common Emotional States:

Rose Quartz: Love and Self-worth

Often considered the quintessential stone of love, Rose Quartz nurtures the heart. Whether you're healing from heartbreak or learning self-love, this gentle pink crystal is a comforting friend.

Citrine: Joy and Abundance

Sunny Citrine, with its vibrant yellow hue, resonates with joy and abundance. It's the stone to turn to when you're feeling down, injecting a dose of optimism into your life.

Amethyst: Peace and Tranquility

For moments when your mind is restless, and your heart feels uneasy, the calming energies of Amethyst can envelop you in a soothing embrace, dispelling anxieties.

Lapis Lazuli: Truth and Self-expression

When words feel trapped or when you're struggling to understand your feelings, Lapis Lazuli can help clear blockages, encouraging honest self-reflection and expression.

Black Tourmaline: Protection and Grounding

In the face of negativity, whether from within or external sources, Black Tourmaline acts as a protective shield, absorbing these energies and grounding you.

Working with Crystals for Emotional Healing:

Intuitive Selection: Trust your feelings when picking a crystal. Which one are you drawn to? Your emotional self often knows what it needs.

Meditative Healing: Hold your chosen crystal close to your heart. Breathe deeply, and imagine its energy interacting with your emotion, bringing about healing and balance.

Crystal Pouch: Carry a pouch of selected crystals. Whenever you're feeling overwhelmed, hold onto them, allowing their energies to soothe you.

Sleep Companions: Place the crystal under your pillow. As you drift off, the stone works with your subconscious, promoting emotional healing even in slumber.

Embracing Emotional Wholeness:

Remember, while crystals are profound tools for emotional healing, they are not substitutes for professional care when dealing with severe emotional issues. They should be used as supportive aids.

Life is a dance of emotions, with its highs and lows. But in every step of this intricate dance, crystals are there, supporting, healing, and uplifting. In their silent, sparkling way, they remind us that emotional wounds can heal, and from pain can emerge profound joy and understanding. So, the next time a storm of emotions engulfs you, let these crystalline wonders be your guiding beacon toward serenity.

CHAPTER 11: CRYSTALS FOR PHYSICAL WELLBEING: ALLEVIATING AILMENTS THE NATURAL WAY

Our physical vessel—the body—is the medium through which we experience life's tapestry. When it's in good health, we often take it for granted, but when physical discomfort arises, it becomes our foremost concern. Crystal therapy, an age-old tradition rooted in the natural world, offers a gentle approach to enhance physical well-being.

How Crystals Interact with the Body

Every atom in our body is in a constant state of vibration. Crystals, with their stable and harmonious vibrational frequencies, can interact with these subtle vibrations to promote physical healing. While science continues to explore the nuances of this interaction, centuries of anecdotal evidence sing praises of the therapeutic properties of crystals.

A Selection of Crystals for Physical Wellbeing:

Clear Quartz: Master Healer

Clear Quartz, often known as the "Master Healer," is thought to magnify the healing energy of other crystals and is frequently used in combination with other crystals for this purpose. It's a versatile stone, beneficial for various physical ailments.

Jasper: Nurturing and Grounding

A protective stone, Jasper is often turned to for its nurturing properties. It can aid digestion, support circulatory functions, and boost the immune system.

Carnelian: Vitality and Motivation

If you're feeling fatigued, Carnelian is your go-to stone. Revered for boosting energy and motivation, it's also believed to support reproductive and metabolic systems.

Amber: Purification and Pain Relief

Amber is not technically a crystal, but fossilized tree resin. Its warm energy is believed to help with pain relief, especially for teething in babies and in arthritis for older adults.

Bloodstone: Detoxification and Blood Health

Aptly named, Bloodstone is traditionally used to cleanse the blood. People believe that it can strengthen the immune system, help the organs detoxify themselves, and enhance circulation.

Incorporating Crystals into Physical Healing Regimens:

Crystal Massage: Gently massaging the body with smooth crystal wands can help to stimulate blood flow and alleviate pain. Remember, always move in a direction toward the heart.

Elixirs: Some crystals can be safely immersed in water to create healing elixirs. Before doing so, ensure the crystal is non-toxic and not water-soluble.

Placement on Body: Placing crystals directly on affected areas can channel their energy to where it's most needed. For general wellness, carrying them in your pocket or wearing them as jewelry can be effective.

Crystal Baths: Immerse yourself in a bath infused with your chosen crystal's energy. Not only is this relaxing, but it's a way to envelop your entire body in the crystal's healing vibrations.

A Gentle Reminder:

While crystals are a fantastic complement to other healing modalities, they should not replace medical advice or treatment. When dealing with serious or ongoing health problems, it is imperative to seek the advice of a qualified medical practitioner.

In the vast universe of natural remedies, crystals shine brightly as a testament to the Earth's healing potential. They remind us of our intrinsic connection to nature and its rhythms. Embracing the gifts of these stones can be a beautiful way to support our physical well-being, alleviating ailments in harmony with the natural world. As you journey forward, may these crystalline allies offer you strength, healing, and vibrant health.

CHAPTER 12: MENTAL CLARITY AND FOCUS: CRYSTALS FOR THE MIND

Amidst the ebb and flow of life, maintaining mental clarity and focus can often be a daunting task. Distractions surround us, both external and internal, challenging our ability to stay centered and attentive. In these moments, turning to the world of crystals can provide a grounding and harmonizing force, helping us navigate mental fog and harness our thoughts effectively.

The Brain's Dance with Vibrations

Our brain is a symphony of electric impulses, a network of neurons firing in synchrony. The vibrational frequencies of crystals are believed to interact with these neural waves, guiding them toward coherence and harmony. By aligning our brain's frequency with that of specific crystals, we can amplify clarity and enhance cognitive processes.

Prominent Crystals for Mental Amplification:

Fluorite: The Genius Stone

Often referred to as the 'Stone of the Mind', Fluorite is cherished for its ability to boost comprehension, concentration, and decision-making. Its myriad of colors is believed to stimulate different parts of the brain, making it a holistic stone for mental enhancement.

Amethyst: Tranquil Thoughts

A crystal of spiritual intuition, Amethyst also serves to calm the mind, aiding meditation and sleep. Its serene vibrations can help dissolve mental distractions and bestow clarity.

Lapis Lazuli: Wisdom and Truth

This rich blue stone has long been associated with the pursuit of knowledge. Lapis Lazuli is thought to enhance intellectual abilities and illuminate the path to truth, making it a choice stone for academics and seekers alike.

Clear Quartz: Cognitive Clarity

Known for its amplifying properties, Clear Quartz can serve as a 'reset button' for the mind. When mental fatigue sets in, this crystal is believed to restore sharpness and clarity.

Tiger's Eye: Grounding Decisions

With its bands of golden and brown hues, Tiger's Eye is a grounding stone, perfect for bolstering confidence and decision-making abilities. It's particularly useful during moments of indecision.

Incorporating Crystals for a Clearer Mind:

Meditation Enhancers: Holding or placing a crystal on your forehead (third-eye region) during meditation can amplify your focus and deepen your practice.

Workplace Allies: Placing stones like Fluorite or Clear Quartz on your desk can help maintain mental clarity during long working hours.

Wearable Wisdom: Crystal jewelry, especially pendants that sit near the throat or heart, can constantly emanate their frequencies, aiding continuous mental clarity.

Dream Enhancers: Crystals like Amethyst under the pillow or by the bedside can promote lucid dreaming and restful sleep, leading to a clearer mind upon waking.

In our dynamic world, the quest for mental clarity is continuous. But with the unwavering energy of these crystalline allies, our journey can become one of heightened awareness and enriched understanding. As you delve deeper into your relationship with crystals, may they serve as beacons of clarity, illuminating your thoughts and guiding your focus. Remember, in the vast landscape of the mind, sometimes all we need is a little crystalline nudge to see the path clearly.

CHAPTER 13: SPIRITUAL ASCENSION: CRYSTALS TO CONNECT WITH HIGHER REALMS

The realm of the spirit is vast, mysterious, and tantalizingly elusive. Throughout history, humankind has sought ways to touch the ineffable, to bridge the gap between the mundane and the divine. In our pursuit of spiritual elevation, crystals stand out as luminous companions, guiding souls toward ascension and enlightenment.

Understanding Spiritual Ascension

Spiritual ascension refers to the evolving journey of one's spirit, transcending the limitations of the physical realm and reaching toward higher planes of existence. It is a process of inner transformation, self-awareness, and expanding consciousness.

Crystals as the Ladders to the Divine

Crystals, with their pure and resonating frequencies, can act as conduits between our earthly experiences and spiritual realms. Their natural lattice structures not only reflect beauty but also embody unique vibrational signatures that align with spiritual energies.

Sacred Stones for Spiritual Growth:

Selenite: Divine Light

Often referred to as 'liquid light', Selenite emanates pure, high-frequency energy. It is believed to open the crown and higher chakras, facilitating communication with guardian angels and spiritual guides.

Moldavite: Cosmic Connection

Formed from a meteorite impact, Moldavite vibrates with extraterrestrial energies. This tektite is renowned for its transformative power, accelerating spiritual growth and opening interdimensional doorways.

Labradorite: Mystical Awakening

With its dazzling play of colors, Labradorite awakens one's inner magic and psychic abilities. It is believed to facilitate transformation and provide protection, particularly on travels that are spiritual in nature.

Angelite: Celestial Communion

Living up to its name, Angelite is believed to enhance communication with the angelic realm. This serene blue stone promotes feelings of peace and interconnectedness with all beings.

Kyanite: Alignment and Ascension

Kyanite is well known for its capacity to automatically align all of the chakras in the body, and it also stimulates the passage of spiritual vibrations through the body. It's especially useful in meditation and dream work.

Engaging with Crystals for Spiritual Journeys:

Guided Meditation: Incorporating crystals in your meditative practices can deepen your experiences. Hold a crystal-like Selenite in your hand or place it on your crown chakra, and visualize its light guiding your spirit upwards.

Sacred Spaces: Creating a sacred altar with spiritually resonant crystals can help anchor higher energies in your space. Spend quiet moments here, connecting and communicating with higher realms.

Wearable Wisdom: Wearing jewelry crafted from these spiritual stones can help maintain a continuous connection with higher energies throughout the day.

Dream Enhancers: Place crystals like Labradorite under your pillow or by your bedside. These can act as gateways to higher dimensions in dreams, enabling astral travels and lucid dreaming experiences.

The journey of spiritual ascension is deeply personal, unique to each seeker. Yet, in the vast expanse of the cosmos, these crystalline companions remind us that we are not alone. They serve as bridges, helping us tread the path of enlightenment, and ushering us closer to the mysteries of existence. As you embark on your spiritual voyage, may these crystals be your guiding stars, illuminating the way to realms beyond imagination. Embrace their energies, and let your spirit soar.

CHAPTER 14: CRYSTALS IN DAILY LIFE: INTEGRATING THEM INTO YOUR ROUTINE

In the vast, shimmering universe of crystals, each stone beckons with a promise— to comfort, to heal, to empower. But how does one seamlessly incorporate these ethereal energies into the everyday rhythm of life? The answer lies in weaving the vibrations of crystals into your daily rituals, turning ordinary moments into pockets of magic and resonance.

Morning Awakenings: Rise with Crystal Energies

Clear Quartz Morning Meditation: Begin your day by holding a piece of clear quartz, a master healer and energy amplifier. A few moments in its company can set a clear and vibrant tone for the day.

Amethyst Under Your Pillow: Known to stimulate dreams and cut through mental fog, keeping an amethyst beneath your pillow can give you a calm and focused start.

Daily Endeavors: Work, Creativity, and Productivity

Fluorite for Focus: Place a fluorite stone on your workstation. Revered as the "Genius Stone", it's known to boost concentration and decision-making.

Carnelian for Creativity: Whether you're painting, writing, or brainstorming, carnelian can ignite a creative spark. Wear it as jewelry or keep it close to your creative space.

Shungite for EMF Protection: In today's digital age, surrounded by electronic devices, Shungite can act as a shield against electromagnetic frequencies (EMFs).

Harmonious Homes: Energize Living Spaces

Rose Quartz for Love: Positioning this stone of unconditional love in the living or bedroom can nurture relationships and create a harmonious environment.

Black Tourmaline for Protection: Keep this grounding stone near the entrance of your home to ward off negative energies.

Selenite for Serenity: Its pure vibrations can cleanse spaces. Consider having selenite lamps or placing selenite wands in corners for a serene ambiance.

Evening Wind Down: Embrace Restful Energies

Lepidolite for Relaxation: This lilac stone, rich in natural lithium, can be your nighttime companion. Holding it can ease anxious thoughts, preparing you for rest.

Moonstone Bath Ritual: Associated with the moon, this stone can turn your bath into a ritual. Place it near your bathtub and let its soothing energies wash over you.

Special Moments: Elevate with Crystal Vibes

Celestite for Spiritual Practices: Enhance your yoga or spiritual routines by creating a circle with celestite stones, allowing its gentle energies to amplify your practices.

Tiger's Eye for Courage: Facing a challenging day? Wear tiger's eye jewelry. Its empowering energies can lend you the courage and resilience you need.

Incorporating crystals into daily life is akin to dancing with the energies of the Earth. It's about finding resonance in moments both monumental and minuscule. Whether you're sipping your morning tea, facing a sea of emails, or drifting into dreams, let these crystalline companions be your guides. By weaving their energies into your routine, not only do you invite balance and harmony but you also turn each day into a luminous journey of connection, discovery, and joy. So, embrace the sparkle, let it infuse your days, and watch how the mundane transforms into the magical.

CHAPTER 15: SPECIALTY CRYSTALS: RARE STONES WITH UNIQUE POWERS

In the crystal realm, while many stones like rose quartz or amethyst might be familiar to most, there exists a subset of gems whose rarity and potency make them particularly special. These specialty crystals, often less commonly found yet profoundly powerful, possess unique energies that can deeply resonate with our being. Let's delve into these exceptional stones, unlocking their secrets and understanding how to harness their potential.

1. Moldavite: The Star-born Stone

Originating from a meteorite impact over 15 million years ago, Moldavite is often referred to as a gem from the stars. With its rich green hue and glassy texture, it's a high-frequency powerhouse. Those sensitive to energies might even feel a warming sensation when holding it.

Usage: Moldavite can be used to enhance spiritual transformation, accelerate personal evolution, and connect with higher dimensions.

2. Phenacite: The High-Energy Enhancer

It is believed that the higher chakras, particularly the third eye and crown chakras, can be attuned to the resonant frequencies of this unusual crystal, which is often transparent or very slightly yellow. Its vibrations can enhance inner visions and stimulate profound spiritual experiences.

Usage: Place phenacite on your forehead during meditation to elevate your consciousness or integrate spiritual insights.

3. Larimar: The Dolphin Stone

Hailing from the Dominican Republic, Larimar, with its dreamy blue hues reminiscent of the Caribbean Sea, is said to embody the energies of water, sky, and the Earth. It soothes, heals, and enlightens.

Usage: Larimar can be worn as jewelry to tap into its calming energies, or used in meditation to connect with inner wisdom.

4. Shungite: The Ancient Purifier

Dating back around 2 billion years, Shungite from Russia is revered for its powerful purification properties. Rich in fullerenes, it's known for neutralizing negative energies and pollutants.

Usage: Place Shungite stones around electronic devices for EMF protection or in water to cleanse and charge it.

5. Tektite: The Cosmic Bridger

Originating from meteoric impacts, Tektites are black or dark brown stones that are believed to strengthen the human energy field. They act as bridges, connecting Earthly energies with extraterrestrial ones.

Usage: Holding tektites during meditation can stimulate inter-dimensional communication and ground spiritual energies.

6. Charoite: The Transformation Crystal

Found only in Russia, this violet gem is renowned for its swirling patterns. It's a stone of transformation, enhancing inner strength, courage, and intuition.

Usage: Wear charoite to overcome fears or use it during sleep to stimulate insightful dreams.

As you venture into the world of specialty crystals, remember that the rarity of a stone doesn't solely define its potency. It's the synergy between your intentions and the crystal's inherent energy that creates magic. Like meeting a wise elder who shares tales from worlds you've never known, these rare gems can offer insights, wisdom, and transformations that are profound.

In embracing these specialty stones, you're not just accessing their unique powers, but you're also honoring the rich tapestry of the Earth and cosmos. Each crystal, be it common or rare, carries within it a story – a dance of elements, time, and energy. So, as you hold or wear these specialty crystals, take a moment to listen to their tales, and let their energies guide you deeper into your own unique journey of discovery and resonance.

CHAPTER 16: CHILDREN AND CRYSTALS: SAFE PRACTICES FOR YOUNG USERS

The soft buzz of a child's energy is analogous to a blank canvas that is waiting to be colored in with the vibrant hues that are acquired via various experiences and interactions. Just as we, as adults, can benefit from the harmonious dance of crystals, so too can our young ones. However, when introducing children to the world of crystals, a careful and considered approach is paramount.

1. The Natural Connection: Children and Earth's Treasures

Children, in their innate innocence and curiosity, have an uncanny ability to connect deeply with nature. They sense the vibrational frequencies of crystals, often more purely than adults. This makes them naturally receptive to the energies of these stones.

2. Starting Simple: Gentle Stones for the Young

For beginners, especially children, it's best to begin with gentle stones that radiate calm and soothing energies.

Rose Quartz: This soft pink stone is known as the stone of unconditional love, and it can assist children in developing sentiments of self-worth as well as kindness toward others.

Amethyst: This lilac stone is excellent for promoting calm and peaceful sleep. Consider placing it near your child's bed or under their pillow.

Citrine: To boost creativity and confidence, this sunny stone is a delightful companion, especially during school projects or artistic endeavors.

3. Safety First: Crucial Tips for Parents

Size Matters: Always choose larger stones that cannot be easily swallowed. Tumbled stones with smooth edges are ideal.

Supervision is Key: While children can hold and explore the crystal, always ensure they're under adult supervision.

Avoid Toxic Stones: Some stones, like Malachite, can be toxic when ingested. Stay informed and always keep such stones out of children's reach.

4. Encourage Exploration: Let Them Choose

Whenever possible, allow children to choose their crystals. They often instinctively pick what resonates best with them. Notice their choices; it can give insights into what they might need energetically.

5. Integrating Crystals in Their Routine

Story Time: Narrate tales about crystals, perhaps about a brave citrine that banishes fears or a wise turquoise that tells ancient stories.

Crystal Crafts: Encourage crafty endeavors like making crystal gardens or painting stones.

Crystal Meditation: Short, guided visualizations, focusing on the energy of a specific crystal, can be a calm and bonding activity before bedtime.

6. Cleansing Crystals for Children

It's just as important to cleanse a child's crystal as it is for adults. Soft methods like moonlight charging or placing them on a selenite plate can be effective. Engage children in the process and turn it into a fun, ritualistic activity.

7. Respect Their Experience

Children may come up with descriptions or feelings about a stone that might seem out of the ordinary. It's vital to honor and validate their experiences. Their perspective, untainted by preconceived notions, can offer fresh insights into the world of crystals.

In a world filled with digital distractions, introducing children to crystals can be a grounding and enlightening experience. It not only brings them closer to nature but also helps them navigate their feelings and energies more adeptly. As guardians, our role is to guide, protect, and ensure that their journey with crystals is both safe and fulfilling. After all, in the heartbeats of these young ones, we often find the purest rhythms of the universe. And with crystals by their side, these rhythms can sing even more harmoniously.

CHAPTER 17: CRYSTAL COMBINATIONS: SYNERGIES FOR ENHANCED OUTCOMES

Nature's symphonies are most beautiful when diverse instruments play in harmony. Similarly, while individual crystals have their unique vibrations and properties, combining them can yield amplified and synergistic outcomes. It's like making a cup of herbal tea – each herb has its benefits, but when brewed together, they offer a complex, rich tapestry of flavors and health advantages.

1. The Magic of Synergy

In the world of crystals, synergy refers to the amplification of energies when two or more stones are used together. This combination can enhance, modify, or even create new energy pathways that cater to specific needs and desires.

2. Combining for Chakra Balancing

By now, you're familiar with the chakra system. Some crystals work exceptionally well in pairs or trios for balancing these energy centers. For instance:

Root Chakra: Red Jasper (for grounding) can be combined with Smoky Quartz (for protection and anchoring) to fortify your foundational energy.

Heart Chakra: Rose Quartz (love and compassion) paired with Green Aventurine (heart healing and luck) can facilitate emotional balance and openness.

3. Intent-driven Combinations

Your intentions play a crucial role in how you might want to combine crystals. Some tried-and-tested pairs based on popular intents include:

Stress Relief: Amethyst (calming) with Lepidolite (soothing and mood-stabilizing).

Mental Clarity: Clear Quartz (amplifying and clearing) with Sodalite (logic and intuition).

4. The Art and Science of Pairing

Complementary Frequencies: Crystals that resonate at similar frequencies can amplify each other's energies. For example, Citrine (abundance) and Pyrite (manifestation) can be a potent duo for attracting prosperity.

Balancing Energies: Sometimes opposites attract. A grounding stone like Black Tourmaline can balance the high-frequency vibes of a Moldavite.

5. Exploring Trios and Complex Combinations

Sometimes, a duo might not provide the holistic energy you're looking for. Trios or even more complex combinations can be the answer. For instance, for comprehensive spiritual protection: Black Tourmaline (grounding), Labradorite (shielding the aura), and Amethyst (spiritual calm) can be a robust trio.

6. How to Use Combined Crystals

Crystal Grids: Lay them out in specific patterns to direct energy flow.

Together on Your Person: Wear them as jewelry or keep them in your pocket.

Meditation: Hold or place them around you during meditation to tap into their collective energies.

7. Not Just Any Combination: The Importance of Personal Resonance

While there are many traditional combinations passed down through ages, the world of crystals thrives on intuition and personal resonance. What works for one might not work for another. So, experiment, feel the energies, and trust your intuition.

8. A Word of Caution

While synergies are powerful, it's essential to ensure you don't overwhelm yourself. Start slow. Introduce one new crystal at a time and observe the energies. Remember, it's a dance, and it takes two (or more) to tango. Find your rhythm.

In conclusion, the journey with crystals is ever-evolving, much like our own personal and spiritual journeys. Combining crystals is both an art and a science, a dance of energies waiting to be choreographed. Embrace the dance, understand the partners, and let the combined symphony elevate you to realms of balance, harmony, and profound joy.

CHAPTER 18: CRAFTING CRYSTAL JEWELRY: WEARING YOUR INTENTIONS

Wearing crystals isn't just a modern trend, but a practice steeped in ancient tradition. From the royal courts of yesteryears to the bustling streets of today, adorning oneself with these natural wonders has been a way to not only showcase beauty but also to harness the potent energetic qualities of these stones. When we intertwine the art of jewelry with the power of crystals, we create a harmonious fusion of intention, style, and energy.

1. The Essence of Wearing Crystal Jewelry

Wearing crystal jewelry allows us to maintain a close and continuous connection with our chosen stone's energies. The constant touch against the skin, especially on pulse points, amplifies the energetic interactions, making the experience more intimate and powerful.

2. Choosing the Right Crystal for Your Jewelry

Intuitive Selection: Just as you'd select a stone for healing or meditation, listen to your intuition. Which stone do you feel most drawn to?

Purpose-driven Selection: If you're crafting jewelry for a specific purpose, such as protection or love, choose stones like Black Tourmaline or Rose Quartz respectively.

3. Types of Crystal Jewelry and Their Benefits

Necklaces: Close to the heart chakra, they can influence emotions and overall energy.

Bracelets: Worn on the wrists, they are great for grounding and protection.

Rings: Touching our fingers, they influence our actions and expressions.

Earrings: Near the head, they can aid clarity, focus, and spiritual connection.

4. Setting Intentions with Your Jewelry

Once you've chosen your crystal and the type of jewelry, it's time to set an intention. Hold the piece in your hands, meditate on your goal, and visualize the crystal absorbing and magnifying this intention. Remember, the jewelry serves as a physical reminder of this purpose each time you wear it.

5. Caring for Your Crystal Jewelry

Just like standalone crystals, your jewelry needs regular cleansing and recharging. Methods include:

Moonlight soaking

Sage smudging

Sound bathing

Ensure to also regularly check the physical settings of your jewelry, ensuring the stones are secure and undamaged.

6. Crafting Your Own: A Journey of Creativity and Connection

Making your own crystal jewelry can be a deeply rewarding process. Selecting the stones, designing the piece, and physically putting it together makes the connection even more personal.

Materials: Invest in quality materials, be it silver, gold, or organic threads.

Design: Think of the wearer. Is it a dainty piece or a bold statement?

Assembly: If new to jewelry making, consider taking a workshop or seeking online tutorials.

7. Gifting Crystal Jewelry

Gifting a piece of crystal jewelry is like giving a part of the Earth's heart. When doing so, cleanse the piece of any energy it might have absorbed and set a general intention of well-being and love for the receiver.

8. The Energetic Dance of Adornment

Wearing crystal jewelry isn't just about the beauty of the piece but the energetic dance that ensues. The crystal resonates, the body responds, and there's a continuous exchange of vibrations that uplifts, protects, and heals.

In the end, crafting and wearing crystal jewelry is a harmonious blend of art and intention. It's a journey where style meets spirituality, where beauty intertwines with purpose. Every time you put on that necklace, bracelet, or ring, remember the Earth from which it came, the hands that crafted it, and the intentions that empower it. Embrace the dance, cherish the connection, and let the crystals amplify the song of your soul.

CHAPTER 19: ENVIRONMENTAL HARMONY: CRYSTALS FOR SPACES AND PLACES

The spaces we inhabit—be it our homes, offices, or even our cars —hold energy. Just as crystals can resonate with our personal energies, they can also resonate with the energies of the places around us. When chosen mindfully and placed strategically, these crystalline wonders can transform our environments, creating sanctuaries of balance, harmony, and positive vibes.

1. The Aura of Spaces

Every space, much like humans, has an aura or energy field. This energy is shaped by various factors - the people who inhabit it, past events, and even the location's natural geomagnetic fields. It's crucial to keep these spaces cleansed and balanced, as they impact our well-being.

2. Selecting Crystals for Your Space

The choice of crystal for a space depends on the purpose:

For Calm and Serenity: Amethyst, known for its calming frequencies, is perfect for bedrooms or meditation corners.

For Energy and Vibrancy: Citrine, with its sun-kissed glow, is ideal for living rooms or workspaces.

For Protection: Black Tourmaline or Obsidian, when placed near entrances, can shield spaces from negativity.

3. Geomancy and Crystal Placement

Geomancy, the ancient art of arranging buildings and spaces harmoniously within their environment, considers the flow of energy or 'chi'. Placing crystals in specific spots, like room corners or near windows, can aid in directing this energy flow positively.

4. Creating Crystal Grids for Spaces

Grids, patterns in which crystals are placed, can amplify a space's energy. For instance, a grid of Rose Quartz in a bedroom can enhance love and relationships, while a grid of Clear Quartz in a study can promote clarity of thought.

5. Larger Crystals: Statement Pieces with Power

Large crystals, often called 'generator crystals', can be central energy hubs for an entire room. Whether it's a towering Amethyst geode in a living room or a substantial Clear Quartz cluster in an office, these majestic pieces radiate energy, influencing vast spaces.

6. Crystals for Difficult Spaces

Some areas, like basements or attics, can harbor stagnant energy. Stones like Smoky Quartz or Selenite can cleanse and rejuvenate such spaces, ensuring no corner of our environment is left energetically neglected.

7. Outdoor Harmony: Gardens and Natural Spaces

Nature is already in a delicate balance, but introducing crystals to gardens or patios can further enhance the serenity. Moss Agate can nurture plant growth, while Shungite can purify water features.

8. Maintaining the Energy of Your Spaces

Just as with personal crystals, those used for spaces need regular cleansing. Larger pieces can be cleansed with sound (like singing bowls), while smaller ones can be bathed under moonlight or smudged with sage.

9. The Transformed Space: A Sanctuary of Crystal Resonance

After introducing crystals to your environment, you might notice subtle shifts. Perhaps the living room feels more welcoming, or the bedroom more restful. These stones, in their silent wisdom, work continuously, harmonizing energies and creating sanctuaries of peace.

To conclude, whether you're looking to energize, soothe, protect, or cleanse, there's a crystal waiting to grace your space. By inviting these pieces of Earth's heart into our environments, we create more than just aesthetically pleasing corners; we create hubs of amplified intentions, grounded energies, and sheer vibrational harmony. Embrace this art of environmental harmony, and let every corner of your world resonate with the symphony of the universe.

CHAPTER 20: COMMON MYTHS DEBUNKED: CRYSTAL FACTS VS. FICTION

Welcome, dear reader, to an enlightening exploration into the world of crystal myths and misconceptions. With the rise in popularity of crystal therapy, there's also been an influx of half-truths, legends, and plain old fallacies. Let's journey together to shine a light on these myths and uncover the sparkling truth.

1. Myth: All Crystals Have the Same Energy

Fact: Every crystal has its own unique vibrational frequency. Just as each of us has a distinctive personality, so too does each crystal. Some, like Rose Quartz, emit nurturing energies, while others, like Citrine, promote vigor and vitality.

2. Myth: Bigger Crystals Are More Powerful

Fact: Size doesn't determine power in the realm of crystals. While larger crystals can influence larger spaces or groups of people, a small, well-intentioned crystal can be just as potent, especially in personal healing.

3. Myth: Crystals Never Need Cleansing

Fact: Just like us, after a challenging day, crystals can benefit from an energetic cleanse. Over time, they may absorb various energies and require purification through methods like smudging, moonlight, or saltwater baths.

4. Myth: Crystals Can Do All the Work Alone

Fact: Crystals are allies and tools. While they can assist and amplify intentions, the actual healing journey requires your active participation, be it through meditation, affirmation, or other therapeutic methods.

5. Myth: You Can't Use Multiple Crystals at Once

Fact: Combining the energies of various crystals can be synergistic. However, it's essential to ensure their energies are harmonious and aligned with your intentions.

6. Myth: Crystals Are Instant Magic Cures

Fact: Crystals provide support and energy alignment, but they don't offer instant fixes. Their benefits manifest over time and in tandem with genuine personal effort.

7. Myth: All Clear Crystals Are Quartz

Fact: While Clear Quartz is the most recognized clear crystal, there are others like Selenite, Apophyllite, and Danburite. It's always good to research or consult experts when identifying crystals.

8. Myth: Synthetically Grown Crystals Aren't Effective

Fact: Lab-grown crystals, in terms of structure and energy, can mirror their natural counterparts. However, some purists believe that naturally sourced crystals, having grown over millennia, carry Earth's wisdom and are more potent energetically.

9. Myth: You Should Never Let Others Touch Your Crystals

Fact: While it's true that crystals can absorb energies, it's also possible to cleanse and reset them. If someone touches your crystal, it won't become permanently tainted. Just ensure you periodically cleanse your crystals.

10. Myth: Wearing Crystals Can Replace Medical Treatment

Fact: Crystals should be used as complementary tools, not replacements for medical or psychological treatments. Always consult with professionals regarding health concerns.

In the world of crystal therapy, as in life, knowledge is power. Being informed, researching, and asking questions can enhance your relationship with these Earthly treasures. As you delve deeper into the crystalline realm, remember to approach with an open heart, but also a discerning mind. After all, the genuine magic of crystals shines brightest when combined with truth, understanding, and intention. Happy crystallizing!

CHAPTER 21: THE FUTURE OF CRYSTAL THERAPY: WHAT LIES AHEAD

Embarking on this crystalline voyage with you has been nothing short of magical. As we approach our journey's horizon, let's peer into the shimmering future of crystal therapy, exploring the innovations and evolving practices that await us.

1. Technological Integration and Crystal Therapy

The melding of technology and traditional crystal healing practices is becoming more prominent. Imagine wearable devices enhanced with specific crystals, not just for their aesthetic beauty but for the energy they imbue. Smart jewelry could potentially monitor physical metrics while also providing the energetic benefits of embedded stones.

2. Crystal-infused Architecture

As our understanding of environmental harmony grows, architects and interior designers are integrating crystals into the very foundations and structures of buildings. Such spaces not only look stunning but are also designed to resonate with specific vibrational frequencies that promote well-being and balance for their inhabitants.

3. Crystals in Space Exploration

It may sound like science fiction, but with humanity's steps into the cosmos, the role of crystals in space exploration is a tantalizing prospect. Crystals might be used for their potential protective energetic qualities in spacecraft and extraterrestrial habitats.

4. Advanced Crystal Elixirs and Integrative Medicine

Modern medicine is beginning to see the merits of integrative approaches. The development of advanced crystal elixirs, made using precise methods and combined with other holistic treatments, may soon become a more commonly prescribed remedy in clinics and hospitals.

5. Virtual Reality (VR) and Crystal Meditation

Picture this: donning a VR headset and finding yourself in a magnificent crystal cave for meditation. As technology evolves, such experiences might offer amplified energy sessions, allowing practitioners to immerse themselves in virtual crystal realms.

6. Eco-conscious Mining and Ethical Sourcing

As our collective consciousness shifts towards sustainability, the demand for ethically sourced and responsibly mined crystals will surge. Provenance will play a critical role, ensuring that our beloved stones are not only powerful but also procured with love for Mother Earth.

7. Community Crystal Grids

Envision entire neighborhoods or cities coming together to create large-scale crystal grids, fostering community harmony and collective intentions. Such endeavors can act as powerful beacons of positive energy, impacting larger groups and territories.

8. Personalized Crystal Diagnostics

In the future, we may see diagnostic tools that, using a combination of biofeedback and energy readings, recommend personalized crystal regimens. Such tailored approaches could ensure more effective and resonant healing journeys.

9. Enhanced Crystal Education

With the rise in interest, more formalized education platforms around crystal therapy may emerge, leading to globally recognized certifications and standards.

10. Evolution of Crystal Frequencies

Just as we evolve, so too do our crystalline companions. As Earth undergoes its shifts, the energetic properties of crystals may also undergo subtle changes, continuously offering new healing potentials.

In this ever-evolving tapestry of life, crystals remain our

steadfast allies, shimmering with promises of growth, healing, and transformation. As we step into the future, hand in hand with these ancient Earth treasures, one thing remains clear: the dance between humanity and crystals is an eternal one, forever moving towards greater understanding, deeper connection, and boundless love. So, dear reader, keep your heart open and your crystals close, for the future is as bright as the most radiant crystal you've ever laid eyes on.

CHAPTER 22: CONCLUDING THOUGHTS: YOUR EVER-EVOLVING JOURNEY WITH CRYSTALS

As we approach the end of our crystalline sojourn, let's take a moment to reflect on all that we've learned. Crystals, with their multifaceted personalities and radiant energies, invite us to engage in a deep, transformative dance with the universe.

1. The Infinite Dance of Energies

It's astonishing how these age-old treasures from Mother Earth interact with our own energies. Every crystal, with its unique vibrational frequency, encourages us to harmonize our inner rhythms with the vast cosmic dance around us. Whether you're seeking emotional healing with a rose quartz or spiritual ascension with a selenite, remember that it's a two-way street. Just as we seek resonance with crystals, they too find resonance with us.

2. Nurturing Your Relationship with Crystals

Your relationship with crystals is like any other; it thrives on respect, understanding, and genuine interaction. Treat each stone not as a mere object but as an energetic entity. Engage with them, meditate with them, and most importantly, listen to them. Their silent whispers carry the wisdom of the ages.

3. The Evergreen Quest for Balance and Harmony

In today's tumultuous world, the quest for balance and harmony is more pressing than ever. And while crystals are powerful allies, they're not magical cure-alls. They guide, amplify, and support, but the true work comes from within. As you integrate crystals into your life, remember to pair their energies with mindfulness, introspection, and proactive efforts toward personal growth.

4. An Invitation to Lifelong Learning

The world of crystals is vast and ever-expanding. Even as you close this book, know that your journey is just beginning. Every interaction, every meditation, and every moment of healing with a crystal will offer fresh insights and revelations.

5. Sharing the Magic

One of the most beautiful aspects of crystal therapy is its communal nature. Share your experiences, insights, and stories with others. The collective energy of a group amplifies the healing and transformative potential of crystals. Perhaps, in time, you'll become a beacon for others, guiding them on their own crystalline journeys.

6. Gratitude to Mother Earth

Lastly, as we bask in the radiant energies of these beautiful stones, let's express our heartfelt gratitude to Mother Earth. For it is she who nurtures and produces these crystalline wonders. As guardians of our planet, it becomes our sacred duty to protect, respect, and cherish her in return.

In closing, may your path shimmer with the radiant hues of a thousand crystals. May every step you take be grounded in purpose, and every challenge you face be met with a heart full of hope and hands filled with Earth's treasures. Remember, dear reader, the universe sings a song of love and unity, and with crystals by your side, you're always in tune. Journey onward, with love and light, and let the dance with crystals be ever joyous and bright.

THE END